Ribbon of Lies, Knife of Truth

Jean Sheldon

Pacific Press Publishing Association
Mountain View, California
Oshawa, Ontario

Design by Ichiro Nakashima

Library of Congress Cataloging in Publication Data

Sheldon, Jean, 1956-
  Ribbon of lies, knife of truth.

  1. Theodicy—Popular works.   2. Seventh-day
Adventists—Doctrinal and controversial works.
I. Title.
BT160.S48   231'.8   81-16880
ISBN 0-8163-0449-1   AACR2

Acknowledgments

Many people have contributed to my understanding of God and thus to this book. But none have inspired me with greater faith in and admiration of God than those whose minds were illuminated by the Holy Spirit. To the Bible writers I owe the basis and substance of my faith in God.

Of those who have helped me understand the Bible better, I am most indebted to an author by the name of Ellen White. As a young teenager she was tormented by misconceptions about God's character. Her search for the truth about God enabled Him to give her a special message to illuminate the Bible and refute Satan's lies that He was not a righteous God.

Anyone who picks up one of her main works can immediately sense her deep concern for God's reputation. Her favorite theme and her unique contribution to theological thought lies chiefly in her harmonious, biblical picture of God. Everything she wrote, whether the theme was salvation or healthful living, was based upon her understanding that the sin problem surrounds Satan's lies about God. No one else in recent Christian thought has written so consistently or so fully about His character.

You will find many of her ideas on these pages, for to her I owe my ability to understand clearly what the Bible says about God. If she were alive today, perhaps I would thank her personally for her contribution to this book. But I really think she would rather that I thank her closest Friend instead.

Thus, because Jesus' revelation of the Father made this book possible, I dedicate these pages to Him.

Contents

Prologue 7

Flashback Eden
Chapter 1 9
Chapter 2 15
Chapter 3 22

Flashback Bethlehem
Chapter 4 29
Chapter 5 34

Flashback Calvary
Chapter 6 41
Chapter 7 51

Flashback New Eden
Chapter 8 59
Chapter 9 66

Epilogue 75

Prologue

The street is fairly quiet. Only the occasional rumbling of cars and the gentle hum of voices interrupts the peace.

Bang! A sudden blast of gunfire shatters the afternoon calm. Faces tighten and lose color as they bend over the victim. Nineteen years old—black male—blood pouring from his mouth—gray casket—flowers, flowers—grave—tears—tears—question: Why?

Some merely shrug and go back home. After all, it's just a typical day in the urban arena.

The rooms are bouncing, laughing, crying, kicking. But that's all one can expect in a pediatrics ward. Bright-eyed Marla announces that her mommy is coming to get her soon. Well, it hasn't been terribly bad in the hospital. The pain—yes, that was tough. But it was fun having all the nurses sign her cast.

In another room Kerry is quiet, staring blankly at the flowers beside his bed. Softly his parents walked in—mother tear-streaked, father with lips pressed tightly together. "Hi, Kerry!" They try to smile.

Kerry stares. "Aaaah!" is all he says.

They try to make conversation. "Kerry, guess what trick Frosty has learned!—John came over yesterday—Your teacher sent you this card. Isn't it pretty?"

But the horrible stare is their only answer.

Numbly they walk out past the blur of white, beyond the antiseptic odors reaching out sterile fingers of despair. In the car Kerry's father bangs his fist on the steering wheel. "He's not my son anymore!" he yells hoarsely. "He's not Kerry! He's somebody else—or nobody at all."

The words fall, then fade into empty, hopeless silence, leaving only painful memories behind. The blond, blue-eyed child dancing home from school—the drunk driver—the scream—the flashing light—the silence—the unending silence—the question: Why?

"Why?" That eternal question nobody can seem to answer, yet everyone tries to. "Why? Why this suffering?"

"Why did my kitty get run over, Mommy?"

"Why do I have cancer?"

"Why did the tornado hit *our* house?"

"Why unemployment?"

"Why poverty?"

"Why? Why? Why?"

Finally the hurt gets too big, the media reporting too common, the question buried too deep beneath mountains of overwork. Apathy pushes the question aside in the blind hope that by shrugging it off today, maybe tomorrow it will get better.

Until it happens to you. And then the bothersome question surfaces to interrupt your busiest period of the day, your happiest possible moment, the dark hour of a sleepless night. "Why? Why? Why?"

The question didn't begin with six million Jews, with black slaves beaten in the fields, or with horror in a Roman coliseum. Back at the beginning, before the earth was created, this very question rose within the heart of God.

"Why? Why this suffering?"

8

Flashback Eden—

Chapter 1

It was the cool part of the evening—that time of the day when shadows reached gently from trees to embrace the earth, when hills smile with changing colors, when nocturnal creatures blend their voices.

This is the part of the day God had anticipated most until now. Ever since He had created Adam and Eve, He had set apart these hours of each day to fellowship with them. Just last evening they had shared with Him one of the surprises He'd carefully hidden for them in nature. He remembered their joyous excitement. Their laughter had bubbled out until all nature seemed to dance and chuckle with them. He remembered—with an ache—how they had run to meet Him.

Majestically, God continued walking through the woods, past a gushing brook, through a meadow. As He approached the tree of life, He began to sing, His rich voice filling space with loving melody.

But tears threatened to blur the song and break it off into a heartrending sob. Tonight they would not come. Tonight only the evening creatures came, and they acted strangely.

He put more tenderness into his song. If only they would come! He wanted them to come with all His aching heart. But they wouldn't come, and He knew why.

They were afraid of Him—their God and Creator. Afraid

of the One who had given them each other in love. Afraid of the One who had talked and walked with them. Afraid of the one who had shown them so much love.

The sobs—could he keep them back?

Why? Why their fear? Yes, they had listened to the serpent. But the serpent hadn't reached out loving arms to them. He had only spoken empty words—lies. God *loved* them; they knew that. Why had they gone away?

Then God's memory traced back across a certain ribbon of separation in time and space.

He had been perfect, with a majestic face one could never forget. His brilliant mind, beautiful personality, and good looks had made him the greatest of God's created beings. He had moved among his friends with such dignity that they all but worshiped him.

His name was Lucifer, meaning "Light Bearer." In his face, words, and actions flashed the awesome light coming from God Himself

That light—blazing brighter than a thousand suns, yet settling down more gently than a mother's caress—was the glory of God. Its power exploded into worlds. Its wisdom organized the harmony of a universe that flowed in rhythm to God's heartbeat. Its presence smashed all barriers to the freedom of God's creatures to think and do. Its love gave all to everyone, asking only to touch off that response in them called love. That light was the intense reality of God's unique Self.

Because God spun all creation on the axis of freedom, He wanted His being to obey Him because His laws were reasonable, to trust Him because they found Him trustworthy, to worship Him because He meant to them joy, love, and freedom. Such spontaneous response could only come from beings who knew God to be this gracious Person. And what better way could they know God than for God Himself to walk among them as a Friend?

So God, whom we now know as the Son, chose to bear the light of His character to His angels, who could in turn bear the light to other beings.

But even this didn't satisfy the Godhead. Why not choose an angel to join with the Son to bear Their light? He would have to be one who summed up all the qualities of goodness God could pour into one being. Who would be better for this than Lucifer?

As they worked together, Lucifer and God's Son became very close friends. They even bore similar names: "Light Bearer" and "Morning Star." Not one creature in all the universe knew God better than Lucifer.

No one but God knew when it began. No one—not even God—knew fully why it began. Slowly, insidiously, it arose like a single yeast cell, then multiplied until it spread throughout and embraced the heart of Lucifer.

What was it? A tiny cell of jealousy that grew into cells of doubt. Doubt about God.

Lucifer wasn't content to think of himself as merely "Light Bearer." He felt so close to God, so intelligent and beautiful, that he began to think of himself as light itself. If he was the light, he reasoned, he should be treated equally with God.

But there the rub came. God—Father, Son, and Spirit— were gathering rather frequently in council. On the blueprint of Their plans a new world was emerging. New creatures were to live there who would think, act, and appear in the very likeness of God Himself. So special was this creation that God would allow none of His created beings, not even Lucifer, to join Them in planning.

Was it fair? Didn't God know who *he* was? Maybe, just maybe, God didn't really love His Light Bearer after all. And if God didn't love His Light Bearer, perhaps He didn't really love any of His creatures. Maybe no one really knew "the truth" about this God of theirs. Was the light Lucifer shared with the angels reality? Or was it a false covering?

If God was not the person He claimed to be and Lucifer was the light, then God had no right to be God and Lucifer should rule the universe himself.

Of course Lucifer's doubts didn't spread that far all at once. But once they started, nothing seemed to stop them. No matter what God did, Lucifer questioned His motive.

When God invited the angels to worship Him, Lucifer felt He was vain and overbearing. When God mentioned His orderly plans for His creatures, Lucifer complained that God was arbitrary and slavish. When God didn't announce to Lucifer immediately that He knew about his doubts, Lucifer decided God wasn't wise enough to know what was going on in His government.

But on the throne an already-aching heart cried out in silent anguish, "O Lucifer, why do you feel this way about Me? I would go to you now, but you must be free to make up your mind without pressure. You have evidence that I am not like you think I am; you've lived saturated in its blazing light. How can you turn from it all?"

Even God, whose intelligent mind probed infinity, whose farsighted wisdom fathomed inerrancy—even this God could not explain fully one mystery: "Why, Lucifer—why are you rejecting Me when there is no reason to do so?"

When freedom could do no more to persuade his brilliant mind, God approached Lucifer with love and reason. "Have I done anything to you that was less than gracious? Do you have any questions that I have failed to answer satisfactorily? Please understand that I have never loved you more. We will still be friends if you will accept the truth about Me."

With tears fogging His voice, God pleaded; and Lucifer saw it so plainly. Only a truly gracious God, freedom-giving and all-wise, could possibly treat him this way. But Lucifer

12

no longer liked that kind of God. It would be too humiliating to admit that he had been wrong and God right. Besides, more and more angels were joining his side and agreeing with him that God was an unrighteous God.

So Lucifer walked away from the One that had given him life, love, and joy. Away from the One whose heart yearned to win him back with love.

Finally, the cells of doubt and jealousy grew and developed into a hardened mass inside Lucifer's mind. Inside, he seemed to shrivel up, turn black with hatred, and die.

And God wept.

"Why Lucifer—why? I can't heal you now. There's nothing more I can do for you; you won't even let My love penetrate."

Then the day came when something had to be done before chaos erupted in heaven. God called all the angels together and tried once more to explain His position. In anguish He watched as the wind of inexplicable rebellion swept through heaven's ranks, carrying away over one third of His angels.

Stepping forward as if he had already arbitrarily decided heaven's fate, Lucifer made an announcement: He would be equal with God! God would simply have to hand him his rights.

Shocked, the loyal angels listened to Lucifer's incredible claim. How could a creature speak arrogantly to his Creator?

His words grieved the sensible mind of God. How could such deception, selfishness, and pride be treated equally with graciousness, humility, and selfless love? For the good of the universe God knew He must act quickly and decisively. "Lucifer, you know the truth about Me—that I am not unrighteous as you have pictured Me. I have done all I can to persuade you to trust Me. Were you deceived, there would be hope, but you know Me better then all My other created beings. You have deliberately turned from the truth, and there is nothing more I can do for you. For the sake of heaven, you must leave."

"And these too?" Lucifer pointed to his fellow rebels.

"Yes." The words came calmly, hiding the sorrow behind them. "These too."

Then a universe which had never before seen force displayed by anyone saw a fist defiantly raised before the blazing light as if to strike God's face. A voice full of hate and force shouted, OK—we'll see who is right! I and my angels will fight against Your Son and His angels and we'll see who has the most power!"

With these words, the rebel who claimed he needed more freedom declared war on God.

The war began, but love is stronger than hatred and prevails. Lucifer soon found himself outside of heaven with all his fellow rebels, wondering what God would do to them now. Would He strike them all dead? Surely He would do something. He looked up, waiting for lightning to strike, but nothing happened. He listened for an angry voice, but there was only silence.

The silence lingered—as deep as the vacuum left in heaven, as penetrating as God's heartbreak, too full for tears. He who had been so beautiful and loving could no longer be called Lucifer, the "Light Bearer." He had now become Satan, God's enemy.

In that pain-filled silence, God's sorrow rose and overflowed into one question, "Why, Lucifer? Why this suffering, this needless suffering?"

Chapter 2

God paused at the tree of life, thinking. He knew where Adam and Eve were. Should He sneak up on them in their hiding place? Never! He wasn't like that. No, He would call them.

"Adam!" He kept His voice firm. "Adam! Where are you?" Solidly the words swept through the trees, across the river, everywhere. To them His voice seemed to strike like a thunderbolt. They were so afraid of Him now. Yet how could they be afraid of their Creator?

And God remembered.

The river's edge, full of rich, dark soil, had been the perfect spot. Here in this shady area beneath the tree of life, God had knelt and begun to move the soil between His fingers. A little water here, a little more earth there— ah, now it was all beginning to respond to His touch.

Now and then God lifted His head to glance at His surroundings. Large trees carried luscious fruits in their boughs. Varicolored flowers lifted waxen faces to the sun. In a vast ensemble, birds trilled and blended in harmony. Nearby, a cheetah padded calmly through the meadow. Gently, a butterfly landed on a flower. The huge cat stopped to study its gauzelike wings—eyes twinkling with delight.

Yes, the garden was perfect now. Six days earlier, the

blueprints ready, God, His Son and the Holy Spirit had begun to build this small new world called Earth. Calmly, with stately dignity, They had uncovered Their plans.

On the first day God had pushed aside the dense darkness with fingers of light. No form of life could exist without light. God smiled as the angels caught the spiritual message: there could be no real freedom, joy, or love without the glory of God's character.

During the second day God's words split the waters apart to form air to breathe. How practical of God, the angels thought. In His orderliness He always makes sure that everything happens in proper sequence. If He had created forms of life first, they would have died immediately without light and oxygen.

The next day lush grass and varicolored flowers carpeted the bare soil of the new world. Small stout green trees stretched their branches toward heaven.

Then, early the fourth morning, a ball appeared against the sky. Warmth sped out of it to embrace the earth, and all nature reached out for its first vigorous hug of sunshine. As the day lengthened, the sun slid down into a silent evening, hiding its face slowly behind trees and hills and kissing the sky good night with a blush upon its cheek. "How God loves beauty!" the angels exclaimed.

As the night meditated deeply, lights appeared—glowing planets, distant twinkling suns, a sphere-shaped satellite reflecting sunshine. The patterns, each one unique, spoke of a God of variety.

On the fifth day God's words set multitudes of feathered creatures aloft on wings. Calling to each other, they soared and wheeled across an endless expanse of blue. As they flew effortlessly, gliding at times on the motion of a wind current, they showed a God who loved freedom.

Then, down in the deep waters, God made mysterious creatures whose varied shapes and colors made the lakes exotic paradises. How like God, the angels thought, to leave nothing empty! If He keeps on like this, He will fill the entire universe with joy and love.

The next day God began calling various creatures into existence. Each had its own unique features. One had a long neck; another, a long nose; and still another, a massive body. Yet each creature's uniqueness fit in proportion with the rest of its body.

Fascinated, the angels watched as each creature rose to its feet and took off across the new world to explore it. One animal with long, hairy arms and legs, in the sheer joy of being alive, shinnied up a tree and swung lightheartedly from branch to branch. Flip-flopping through the air, he caught a branch and made it dance with himself.

From a distance God watched the creature with a twinkle in His eye. Delighted chuckles burst from the observing angels. No matter how dignified or awesome their Creator seemed, His humor seemed to surface and dance like the sparkles on the surface of a river.

As afternoon approached, God seemed to ponder a moment. Nothing was lacking in this world now. Every need and joy had been supplied. Yet—was it really complete? Or was there something more He could do? Yes, there was!

He knew they'd love it. He would plant a garden for their home. Carefully God walked, as if staking out the most beautiful spot on the planet. Here He planted His favorite tree; there, His most luxuriant flower. Over by the river a vine began to climb the bank. Near a lake He formed a sloping hillside on which one could sit and meditate. He would give them space to do all that their imaginations could come up with.

It was like frosting on a well-made cake—or maybe like ice cream on the frosting on the— No, it was like fudge topping on the ice cream on the frosting on the cake! Joy

17

upon joy, love upon love—rich with all that God could give of Himself.

But now God moved to His favorite spot beside the river. Kneeling at its edge, He began to knead the clay with His fingers. In silent admiration, a universe watched as God formed another creature. Something about the way He worked marked this creature as uniquely set apart from the others He made.

With the gentleness of a mother and the eagerness of a father, God formed a son. A son sculptured in His own likeness, with the power to procreate sons and daughters after his likeness. A son with a mind that could also plan and think and create. A son who could study and grasp fathomless depths in the ocean of His love. A son totally free to choose for himself whether or not he would acknowledge God as his Father.

He would spend the evening hours with this son. Together they would walk through the garden, talk their hearts out and sing in the loving unity of a family. For this son would open the entire library of His creation, to help in studying the truth about Himself. *His* son would be dressed with the light coming from Himself.

The sculpturing finished, God stood up and studied the silent form lying at His feet. He would be perfect—brilliant, handsome, free—with the capacity to give and receive love unselfishly.

Then, in sacred love, God knelt once more beside the lifeless creation. Stretching out His arm as if to embrace the body, He placed His mouth upon the body's mouth and breathed into it a part of His own life. The chest swelled, the eyelids flickered, and suddenly Adam looked up into the face of His Father-God bending over him. Overwhelmed, the angels studied the scene. This God of theirs did not merely sit on His magnificent throne ordering His universe from a distance. This God longed to come close to His creatures—to embrace them with His love and to treat them as His friends. This God's breath was the very breath of fellowship.

But there must be more than just one being like this one whom God called Adam. By himself Adam would not be complete; he would not be able to do all that he had capacity to do.

The angels watched as God and Adam went for a walk. "Adam," they heard God say, "since this world is yours to take care of for Me, all these animals are under your care too." They came forward in pairs as God called them. The large man held or gently touched each creature as he decided what their names would be. With a knowing smile, God watched as Adam studied the animal with growing concern.

"Father-God," he asked, "why do all these animals have mates, and I do not? There is no other creature anywhere like me!"

To Adam's bewilderment, God's face lighted up. "I could have made a partner for you from the beginning, but I created you free. I would never force you to love and cherish someone you didn't care for. But if you want me to make someone especially for you, I'd love to do it!"

"Would you—please?"

Shadows were reaching out across the landscape as God awakened Adam and introduced Eve to him. Adam stood and gazed in temporarily speechless wonder at this breathtakingly beautiful counterpart of himself. How enchantingly lovely she was! Her eyes—soft, yet sparkling—caught the rays of the lowering sun and reflected them warmly back to him. Her lips were red as a rose and as soft as its petals. Could God have made them more lovely? She seemed to Adam to be a special part of himself. But then, since God had taken a rib from Adam's

19

side to make her, she *was* part of himself. How he longed to love her—to give her the best of himself!

Eve felt that irresistible wooing of selfless love. How good God was to make her and then give her immediately to someone who would love her and whom she could easily love. How strong and handsome Adam looked. Yet there was something indefinably gentle about him that told her she would always feel safe with him. Here was one in whom she could find both freedom and fulfillment. Her eyes fixed on his, and she let his gentle love draw her into his arms.

The angels drew close to that wedding as God brought Adam and Eve together in His love. Their union revealed that intimate love that seemed to characterize the heart-longings of a God who desired to give all of Himself—His love, joy, and peace—to His creatures.

Now the sixth day was over. Golden bands of a warm setting sun gave a final embrace to Adam and Eve as God left them alone, satisfied. What more could He say about Himself? What were His intelligent creatures thinking now about Satan's lies?

Suddenly a shout was heard on a distant planet. Then another shout—a shout of victory—vaulted up and across the heavens. Then still another shout, and another, until the universe resounded and overflowed with ringing joy!

Angels from every corner of heaven blended their voices in singing a spontaneous and joyful anthem. Higher and higher, fuller and fuller, the music swelled, until every loyal creature God had made joined in the pattern of perfect praise.

"God, You have done it!" they shouted. "You've shown us how perfect, wise, and loving You are. You have demonstrated Your deep concern for our freedom and dignity. God, Satan must be wrong about You. Because of all the evidence we've seen that You are not as he has claimed, we trust You. With all our hearts, we worship You!"

As the earth's golden sun sank into peaceful rest and one by one the stars came sparkling from their hiding places, a gentle, deep voice swept through the vast amphitheater of praise:

"Let's rest now. Six day I have worked and labored in love, and I have shown the truth about Myself. Let's rest from the dark days of controversy and the struggle for righteousness. Rest in My love, and within that rest find a celebration of joy."

Chapter 3

God lingered at the tree of life, wishing that the pleasant memory could remain in His mind forever. If only the tranquillity of that first day of celebration had never been marred. If only Adam and Eve had not—

His sigh poured out—like a cup of sorrow filled too full—into the intense stillness. Adam and Eve had not answered His call. They had responded instead to another's call to distrust their God.

Yes, they had been warned about Satan. In amazement they had listened to reports of his rebellion against God. How, they wondered, could anyone say such terrible things about their gracious God? How could anyone believe that their God was arbitrary, forceful, and selfish?

But now, in spite of the warnings, they had succumbed to Satan's charges. Even God's most beautiful gift—His gift of time—had not kept them from sin.

Because that gift memorialized all that God had revealed about Himself during creation week, God had given it to them to remind them of the truth about Himself. He called His gift of time the Sabbath. After the first day of rest and celebration, God found Adam and Eve enjoying the evening's stillness. There God repeated to them His invitation to join Him in fellowship one day each week, that they might know Him better.

Well He knew the risks He ran that evening in giving them the Sabbath. Well He knew that over this day—this memorial of His answers to Satan's charges—the final battle of Satan's war against God would be fought. This memorial of God's love would be twisted by Satan into a burdensome command—arbitrary and legalistic. To the generations in earth's final days it would seem to confirm every lie about God that Satan had ever uttered.

Because of these misconceptions, another memorial of time would be erected. But it would memorialize only one event in the process of God's vindication—the resurrection of His Son—and thus would not include all of the truth about God. This substitute memorial would set forth to the world a god of force and cruelty. Only a small group of people would in the end seek to correct the misunderstandings of God and His Sabbath.

Yet in spite of all that God forsaw, He gave Adam and Eve this special gift. As He spent the next Sabbath with them, every corner of earth seemed filled with praise. "God," the couple wondered, radiant with His love, "why should anyone believe that You are forceful and unreasonable?"

With the eagerness of teachable students, they waited for His answer. "There is no reason," He responded quietly, "no reason at all."

How enthusiastically they studied the truth about God! And God wished that they could go on learning forever. But in the middle of the garden was the tree that He had permitted Satan to use as a pulpit from which to preach his side of the story. In that tree rested one of the most beautiful creatures God had created. And in that dazzling, brilliant creature lurked the sly, evil Satan.

To that tree the unsuspecting Eve came one day, trusting and confident. No one had ever tried to deceive her before. No one had ever played games with her mind. Like

23

a child, she was as open as a lily in full bloom.

"Oh," crooned the dazzling creature from his lofty height, "is it true that God has said you are not to eat the fruit of *any* tree in the garden?" He appeared puzzled. "I know God is very loving; surely He wouldn't be that arbitrary!"

"Oh no, of course not!" replied the loyal Eve. "God didn't say we couldn't eat of *any* tree. There's just one tree we're not to eat from—*this* tree. God said that we would die if we ate fruit from this tree, the very day we ate it."

"You're intelligent and beautiful," said the creature smoothly. "Surely you've discovered already that God doesn't always mean what He says. Actually He knows that the fruit of this tree would make you so wise that you would be equal with Himself. You know how eager He has seemed to teach you the truth about Himself? Well, you really can't know the truth about God unless you are God, and you can't be God unless you eat this fruit. So if you want to know the truth about God, eat this fruit. You won't really die if you do. His words were just a threat to keep you from this wonderful tree.

"You see, Eve," the voice flowed on without a ripple, "if God had *your* best interests at heart and wasn't so overly concerned with His own reputation, He wouldn't mind if you ate this delightful fruit. But at heart God is a bit selfish and arbitrary. You can't trust Him to always tell the truth."

In a flash, Eve remembered the beautiful garden God had made for them, the delightful wedding ceremony, the love-filled walks with God, the things she'd learned about God just last Sabbath. But now all this seemed overcast by a gray shadow, mysterious and full of doubt. It must have been false, meaningless, unreal. Besides, how could God fault her for eating something that would only help her know Him better?

She grasped the beautiful fruit—the fruit of Satan's

24

lies—and ate it. Such lovely food, such wise-sounding truth must be shared. Higher and higher she filled her arms and then, like a deer, ran swiftly to Adam.

Adam saw her coming. Never before had she looked so beautiful, with her long hair flowing back in the wind and her body moving in rhythm with his own heartbeat. Her face, picking up the color from the fruit in her arms, seemed to glow.

But the fruit—where had she gotten it? Surely she hadn't been to the tree!

"Yes, Adam it's from the tree. Isn't it lovely?—Why Adam? What's wrong? Don't you love me anymore?"

"Yes, of course, Eve, I've never loved you more! But don't you remember what God told us?"

"Oh, but Adam! I wish you could have heard him! The creature in the tree told me that God didn't actually mean what He said about our dying if we ate the fruit. *This* fruit will enable us to know more about God. We'll really know the truth about Him. We'll even be equal with Him because of the fruit."

"What is this truth about Him you're talking about?"

"Adam, the creature said that God is mainly concerned about His own reputation and doesn't always tell the whole truth. And you know, Adam, I'm really beginning to believe it. I really feel like maybe God has been playing games with us and doesn't really care about us!"

"Eve, Eve, how can you believe that? God has done nothing but love us! And yet, how can I do without you? Surely God doesn't expect me to give you up! He made you for me. And—well—maybe in some ways the creature was right about God. Maybe God hasn't completely leveled with us. After all, you're still all right, Eve."

Adam, too, clutched the fruit of Satan's lies and ate it.

The fruit, glittering and tasty, represented a charge against God that, unless answered, would mean absolute rebellion and chaos throughout the universe. Satan had insinuated that God was a liar. Was he right? Had God lied when He told Adam and Eve that they would die if they ate the fruit? What did it mean to die?

The charge weighed heavily on the mind of God. How could He prove His honesty and the righteousness of His government? How could He show what He had meant by His words, "You shall surely die"? He could let Adam and Eve die to show His truthfulness. But would that answer all the questions?

In horrified silence the angels watched as their gracious God, with heartbroken reluctance, withdrew His light from Adam and Eve. Without that light, how could they truly live? How could they know God?

Slowly, sinister fingers of darkness crept out and hovered over the earth. Like black clouds, they encircled the distrustful pair in fear. All nature mourned the loss of God's light. Although the natural light of the sun still shone, the light of God's love and presence no longer beamed on the earth.

His heart aching, God had withdrawn that light. If He had not, the consequences would have been terrible. Distrust of God could never coexist with the intensity of His glory. If God had let His light remain, it would only torture Adam and Eve and finally consume them.

Only no one would ever understand why. To the universe, Satan would have seemed right in claiming that God was cruel. God would have seemed an avenging destroyer who had consumed Adam and Eve in unreasonable anger. This had been one of the very reasons God had not allowed Satan and His followers to be destroyed earlier. And this is why He would not let Adam and Eve be destroyed now.

Now, someone must answer the questions that had been raised about God. Adam and Eve had only been deceived. They hadn't lived as closely to God as Satan had. They hadn't come to know God as Satan had known Him. If God should give them another chance, would they change their minds about Him? Would they let the truth heal them and set them free to enjoy God's light once more?

They would if someone came to demonstrate that truth to them. That someone would have to be equal with God, because only God could reveal the truth about God. And He would have to come in human form. Otherwise His dazzling light would overwhelm and destroy them.

God and His Son meditated on Their plans. Long before, along with the blueprint for the now-cursed planet, these plans had been carefully laid out. In these plans a new Adam would rise to take the fallen Adam's place.

Whereas the fallen Adam had decided that God was unloving, the new Adam would show only a God of unselfish love. Whereas the fallen Adam had failed to trust and obey God, the new Adam would demonstrate His trustworthiness and the correctness of His laws. Whereas the fallen Adam had decided that God had apparently lied in saying that sinning would automatically bring death, the new Adam would prove His honesty by dying a death of complete separation from—

No! God's thoughts broke off sharply, and He bent His head under a heavy load of anguish. "The new Adam will be My Son, My own beloved Son! How can I let Him die that horrible death of absolute separation? How can I bear to see Him—"

"I understand, Father." His Son's voice was gentle.

"But why, Son? Why this suffering for *anyone*, let alone you? But there is no other way unless I let Adam and Eve die. Yet that would not answer all the questions about Us. And besides, I want to save them. Oh why, why did they turn away from Me? Why, when I love them so much?"

"I love them, too, Father. I'm willing. It will be hard, but someday all will be right again."

"Yes, Son. Someday"—and a smile arched up to meet God's tears—"someday the questions and the doubts about Us will all be answered."

The sun slipped gently behind a tree as if trying to hide its face from the Form bowed beneath the tree of life, bathed in tortured memory. At length, God stood and began walking toward Adam's hiding place. *He would find them!*

Of course, He would have to let them know how terrible their sin was. They would have to leave the garden and thus His close presence. But that would not be the end. He would tell them about the One who would come to finish showing them the full truth about Himself.

They must know that God had not forsaken them. He still loved them with all His breaking heart. They were still His children—disobedient, yes—but His children nonetheless. And He would not take everything away from them. Although they would have to leave the garden, they would still have something to take with them.

For the gift of the Sabbath would remain a memorial to the God they had once worshiped face-to-face in light and joy. Throughout their lives it would return each week as a gentle visitor to remind them that God was not the kind of person Satan had made Him out to be. Through worshiping God on His Sabbath, they would be reminded that though they suffered now, God suffered with them and sought to win them back. Even though Adam and Eve had run away from God, the Sabbath would run after them to persuade them that God had not changed nor given up on them. There was still another chance.

As the sun bowed its head upon the eve of earth's saddest day, God called again, "Adam! Adam! Please come to Me!"

Chapter 4

Musty and dark, the barn offered its shelter to the two weary travelers who had searched so long for a place to rest. The light of small lamps flickered against the walls and danced with the shadows. Here among the animals, a child was born—a child of royal blood destined to forever change world history.

Joseph, the pregnant women's husband, spread out the dusty straw on the floor and made her as comfortable as he could. While Mary struggled in labor, Joseph got the water ready, set out long cloths, and waited.

Minutes passed as Mary gasped painfully. Suddenly a sharp cry rang out through the darkness and awakened the sleepy animals in their stalls. A son was born! Cleaning the wee infant, Joseph wrapped Him in the long bands of cloth and laid Him gently in a feeding trough filled with straw.

But the child's real Father watched from a distance. This child was His Son—His own unique Son! Tiny and fragile now, He lay in crude surroundings. And He was so far away! But the distance between Them seemed to span the distance between God and man.

Quickly, the Father traces back to that evening when it had been His heartbreaking duty to tell another son—a son He'd made in His image—good-bye. In that moment the distance between them had seemed to widen into a yawning chasm. For more than forty centuries God had tried to span that distance with offers of reconciliation.

Eagerly He had tried in every possible way to remind Adam and his sons how much He loved them and longed to have them back. Nature still reflected His light, though that reflection was gradually fading. Once a week the Sabbath still reached out across the distance with timeless revelations of Himself.

But there must be something more—something tangible to remind them of a God they could no longer see. They needed a symbol to represent His Son, who would come in person to reveal the truth about Himself.

God chose the most helpless of all His creatures to be the symbol. A lamb, innocent and unobtrusive, would continually point them ahead to the God—also gentle and unobtrusive—who would become a man in order to show them His character.

But they would see more in the lamb than God's gentleness. In the garden Satan had lodged a most terrible charge against God. "God lied to you," he had said to Adam and Eve, "when He told you that you would die if you ate the fruit."

Would they die? Should they die?

To the angel it didn't look as if Adam and Eve would die. They had lost God's light, and eventually they would die that natural death resulting from sin's ravages of the body. But they could still be raised from that death. What about that eternal death of separation from God that Adam and Eve had been warned about? Would they die that death from which there was no resurrection? Or would Satan be proved correct that God had lied?

Before they left the garden, God told Adam and Eve that someone would come to die not only the common death of sinners, but also that final death that results from being totally separated from God. Someone would take their place to show that eternal death is the natural result of sin—of choosing to separate from the Source of life.

Someone would die who was like a lamb. And to help them to remember this, God asked Adam and Eve to kill a lamb when they sinned, confessing their sin over it. Because the final death would be the natural result of sin, Adam and Eve understood that the lamb, and thus the One to come, would receive sin's full results. God would not personally destroy His Son.

The first time Adam raised his knife to slay an innocent lamb, he felt heartlessly cruel. Baby animals are so cute. Why not a full-grown sheep? Why a cuddly lamb?

The angels had asked a similar question of God: "Why Your Son—Your beautiful, loving Son—the One Who is equal with Yourself? Why must You, God, bear the results of sin? Why not one of us?"

"Who else," God had returned, "could reveal the truth about God except God?"

The first lamb lay lifeless in its own blood. Adam and Eve wept. Angels cried out, "Does it have to be this way?"

"Yes," came God's quiet answer; "there is no other way."

But deep within God's heart a question fought its way up from the depths of God anguish to the heights of His love. It was a question for which there really is no answer. "Why, Satan? Why have you caused this suffering?"

Then one day it happened. Out in the fields two of Adam's sons came to worship God. One came with a lamb. The other brought fruit from his own trees. Cain would honor God his own way. He would illustrate the problem of sin by trying to gain God's blessing without the suffering of a lamb. Without the suffering of *the* Lamb. Besides, was it his fault that his parents had accepted Satan's lies about God?

31

But the sin Cain blamed on his parents was also his own. For in his mind, he too had decided that God was unreasonable and cruel. When God failed to accept his offering of fruit, Cain raised a clenched fist toward heaven—reminiscent of Lucifer's gesture—and shouted, "It's not fair for God to reject my offering!"

As he drew out a knife, his arm suddenly froze as he heard God's calm voice: "Cain, why are you angry? Why must you rebel against Me? If you had done what was right, wouldn't I have blessed you? Please accept the truth about Me."

Yet the truth about God necessarily involved the truth about Cain. Enraged, Cain rejected both truths. If he could have, he would have plunged a knife into the very heart of God. But since he couldn't, he chose the person who most clearly resembled God—his brother Abel—and murdered him.

Cain's knife, glittering in the sunlight, seemed indeed to pierce the heart of God. Well He had known how men would kill each other. And well He knew that the tortures and sufferings of the future would nearly exceed human imagination. There would be the horrors of Roman bloodshed, a tragedy of repeated religious persecutions, the needless tyranny of Hitler, the cruel slaughtering of Vietnamese and Kampucheans. And all these did not even include the grim toll of disease, accidents, starvation, and natural disasters.

Well God knew that Satan would point to these horrors—these horrors *he* had caused—and lead God's created beings to blame Him for them all.

More than this, Satan would someday cause it to be preached from countless pulpits that God plans to mercilessly condemn the wicked to an eternal living hell, worse than all the tortures of the past combined. To his lie, "You will not die," would be added an insane description of the punishment of sinners—his monstrous lie!

This senseless blood staining the ground, this meaningless treachery, was the beginning of a heartwrenching history of sorrow and suffering. Gladly would God have turned from it all; gladly would He have allowed it to end. One intense and total unleashing of His glory and sin would be no more.

But the questions about God would have remained unanswered. Such a solution would have destroyed the freedom of the unfallen beings of the universe, who needed to have their questions about God answered in order to worship Him intelligently. Satan would have appeared to be right in his charge that God was at least partially cruel and arbitrary. In fear, not in love, the rest of the universe would henceforth have worshiped Him.

Only suffering, it seemed, could keep the universe free. Only suffering could answer the questions about God. Only the horrible suffering of His Son could prove Satan wrong and God right.

In the intense sadness following Abel's death, angels pondered truth and error. Why was it righteous Abel who died instead of disobedient Cain? Deep within their hearts, even as the tears flowed, the question remained: Why this suffering?

3-R.O.L.

Chapter 5

Bending over Mary, Joseph adjusted the straw. Frequently he looked at the tiny newborn already asleep and then at his tired but contented wife.

Suddenly the wide door swung open, and several men bounded in. Mary gasped. The baby awakened and began to cry. Joseph stepped protectively between the men and Mary with her newborn son.

But then he stopped. These men didn't look dangerous. They looked more like ordinary men—like shepherds. When they saw the newborn they smiled.

"We were out guarding our sheep," panted one of the men, "and talking about the Messiah. You know, everybody thinks He's soon to come. Well, suddenly a being appeared above us surrounded by light. We were so terrified that we fell to the ground."

"All I could think of," exclaimed another, "was that God had decided to devour us in His wrath!"

"But the being seemed to understand our fears," said a third shepherd. "He said, 'You must not be afraid any longer. Look! I have good news for you that will bring great joy to everyone. This very day in David's city, the One has been born who has come to save. He is the Messiah—the Lord.' "

"He gave us clues as to how to find Him," the first

shepherd added, pointing at the infant. "We were told He would be wrapped in strips of cloth and lying in a feeding trough."

"But do you realize," the third shepherd broke in again, "the being called Him 'Messiah—the *Lord*.' That means that this baby is God! God—here in our presence. God—*with us*!"

Far away—and yet, not far away—the baby's real Father smiled at the shepherd's words. "Immanuel, God with us!" At last God was no longer so far away from His truant children. God was with them and yet not only with them—He was *one* of them.

Awe-filled angels were still pondering the unexpectedness of it all. Just when most of the people seemed no longer to care about God, just when it seemed God could never win them back, He had given them Himself in His Son. Amazed they had watched God's Son give up His ability to move freely about the universe and descend into the prison of human flesh. How could God, who had known so much freedom, give it up just to be with His fallen sons and daughters? How could Satan claim that God was unwilling to sacrifice for His creatures?

God smiled again. It would be worth the price. For so long He had missed being with them. There had been few human beings He had been able to get close to.

That thought reminded Him of Abraham. His close friend Abraham! He had been one on the earth who knew God so well that they could reason together face-to-face. How God cherished the memory of Abraham's hospitality to Him out there by his tents under the oaks of Mamre!

The stifling heat had swirled up with an occasional dust devil that afternoon. Abraham sat in the door of his tent gazing out at the shimmering heat waves, glad to be in the shade.

In the distance he thought he saw three figures dancing

with the waves, but perhaps it was merely a mirage. No, there were three men coming toward him, probably hot, dusty, and tired. Even in the heat he ran toward them.

With joy God remembered the warm graciousness of His host. How gratified He was by this man who seemed so much like Himself! Such a carefully prepared meal could not be turned down. After washing His feet in the cool water Abraham provided, God sat down to eat. Afterward, as mealtime guests always did, He conversed with His host. God felt so happy to be talking to a human face-to-face. It was almost like those evenings so long ago when He had walked and talked with Adam and Eve.

As Abraham walked with Him to the road, God opened His heart and they talked, Friend to friend.

"Abraham," God said, "I may have to destroy Sodom and Gomorrah over there in the valley. But I will make sure before I do that the people have gone so far from Me that there's nothing more I can do for them."

Abraham remembered his nephew Lot who lived there. He remembered how gracious and fair he'd always known God to be. "God," he asked, his concern for God's reputation burning bright, "What about the righteous people living there? You wouldn't destroy the righteous along with the wicked, would You? Surely You wouldn't! You are righteous. God, shouldn't the judge of the earth do what is right?"

How correct Abraham was! Those words seemed to ring across the heavens, declaring that all was not lost on earth. God did have one friend to whom He could entrust His reputation.

Abraham had not been God's only friend on earth. There had also been Moses. What a man, that Moses! Here too was someone God could reason with about His character. Here was someone who could even see a portion of His glory.

What a beautiful day that had been on Mount Sinai! God had set Moses in a cave, covered him with His hand, and let Him see as much of the light of His goodness as Moses could endure in his sinful body. If only more had been like Moses and Abraham. So few were, even among God's chosen people, the Israelites.

With a heavy heart God remembered those forty pain-filled, needless years that Israel had tramped the desert sand in petulant rebellion. How many times God had rushed to her rescue. How often He had resorted to firm discipline just to get her attention.

Yet never had He left her completely to her own re-sources, even though she had repeatedly complained that He couldn't be trusted. Instead He fed her with food from heaven, provided cool water for her to drink, led her by a fluffy pillar of cloud during the day, and wrapped warm arms of fire around her at night.

Early in her travels God asked her leader Moses to build a special tent just for Him. "I want to live right among the people," He said. "I want to get as close to them as possible."

Together on Mount Sinai they had shared building plans, and soon Moses had the tent constructed. But it wasn't enough. With clogged ears and hearts, the people refused to listen to Him. With haunting pleas God stretched out loving arms to them. But instead of coming to Him, they drifted farther and farther away.

Disastrous days followed, when everyone did what he decided was right. After every few years of peace, God had let them go into captivity or permit some other form of discipline, in order for them to discover that their false gods didn't really love them.

Finally God was able to find a person He could speak through: Samuel. Ever since Samuel had been a small child, He and God had worked together. His first direct

words to God—"Speak; Your servant is listening"—
seemed to characterize his work as a prophet. Through
Samuel, God had decreased the distance between Himself
and His people.

One day the people told Samuel they wanted a king like
every other nation. How well God would remember the
night Samuel fell on his knees, crying, "Lord, they've
rejected me!"

"No, Samuel." God's reply sounded hollow, as if a part
of His heart were missing. "They haven't rejected you;
they've rejected Me."

The hurt, though centuries old, now seemed only to
intensify in God's mind. Would they ever want His
authority—gracious and liberating? Didn't they know that
a king would become tyrannical, exacting heavy taxes
from them and making them his slaves? How could they
reject freedom, prosperity, love, even national
greatness—all that could be theirs if they let their gracious
God be their king? Would they ever learn the truth about
Him?

The ribbon of Satan's lies about God seemed to stretch
farther away in dark rebellion. Even though a few good
kings had rolled that ribbon partly back up, many evil kings
rolled it out still farther, until it stretched out to a
heartbreaking distance. And God's people followed that
ribbon away from a correct understanding of His character.

Other gods took the place of the Father-God. Other
gods, cruel and enslaving, demanded child sacrifices,
brutality in worship, and promiscuity which degraded
people's bodies to the level of mere feelings. Finally, in the
northern part of Israel, the separating ribbon of satanic lies
rolled out so far that the angels wondered if God would
ever win His people back.

Nevertheless, in the middle of all this darkness, God

could claim that one man, named Hosea, knew Him. In fact, Hosea identified with God so completely that he could reveal in his own life the passionate love and ardent devotion God felt for His people.

"Hosea," God said to him one day, "go downtown to a place where all the religious prostitutes are and get one for your wife."

The incredible command stirred the angels. How gracious was their God, who—though infinitely pure—would stoop as low as necessary to reach His people. Hosea did as God requested, and the story became more than romance. It became the story of a broken heart—God's heart. A story of the God who wanted Israel for His wife.

Hosea's wife didn't stay with him. She ran away to take up again her former way of life, just as Israel had run away from God. "Hosea," God said, "go buy her back—woo her unto yourself again. For I am trying to show Israel that I want to win her back from other gods."

But Israel didn't care about the story of Hosea or about God's love. Finally the ribbon unrolled all the way, leaving God helpless to do anything more for Israel as a nation.

The heartbreak of years, the anguished sobs of infinite love swelled up in God's heart like a towering breaker at high tide. Finally came the agonized plea, "How can I give you up, O Ephraim! How can I hand you over, O Israel!" Hosea 11:8, RSV. But the cry went almost unnoticed on a planet too fully attuned to the din of Satan's lies to really hear.

Then the southern part of Israel ran away from God to other kingdoms. Finally, God chose to allow them to be taken captive. When He restored them to their own country again, they determined to quench their rebelliousness. They would obey God. Yes, they would obey God at all costs.

With exactness they made rules, rules, and still more

rules. Every law God had given them they spelled out in minute detail. But the real God was not in those external human exactions, and their god became a cruel judge— ruthless and unfeeling. And somewhere in his hellish shadows, Satan gloated over the wide acceptance of his caricatures of God.

Recently, questions too obvious to be ignored had haunted the minds of unfallen angels. Could this planet ever come to know the truth about God? Would the separation of rebellion be eternal? God's glory had long been clouded by the darkness of superstition and error. How could God get through without His light proving too overwhelming for eyes accustomed to the darkness?

Now, looking down at the musty barn, God smiled on His Son—still equal with Himself, though now a human being. Those tiny baby hands—were they really God's hands? Those tiny lips and baby eyes, that small body wriggling in the hay—could this infant be God?

The final part of the shepherds' story could be heard coming from the barn: "And then there were many beings, full of light. Light filled the sky and streaks of it bounced off the grass. If only you could have heard them sing! Louder and louder the song swelled until we felt lost in its immensity. 'Glory to God,' they sang, 'Glory to God in the highest and peace to all on earth with good will.' "

The night seemed strangely silent after the shepherds left. Darkness flooded the barn. The baby slept.

Soon the long, dark ribbon of lies would be cut by the knife of truth. Now God would be living among His people in the form of His Son, showing them the real truth about Himself.

Like a flashing knife, God's truth raced out to begin the work of cutting through the dark ribbon of Satan's lies. It raced out with the message: At last He has come— Immanuel, God with us!

Chapter 6

In great pain the bent form—pale and haggard—staggered slowly up the hill. On the brow of that hill instruments of torture would soon raise their bloodstained spires to the morning sky.

Behind Him, sweating and breathless, a powerfully built man labored under the weight of a cross. Beside Him clanked the Roman guards, whose darting eyes noted His every muscle twitch. Their prisoner could not be permitted to escape. But the prisoner was too exhausted to run. Besides, He had no desire to do so.

Behind them all surged the angry mob—violent and malicious. Their jeers and curses seemed to splatter against His back, trickling down it along with the blood from a recent scourging. "Jesus!" they taunted in unison. "Criminal! Criminal! Crucify Him! Crucify Him!"

Finally the crowd stopped, and the soldiers laid Him on the cross. Quickly one grasped His feet to hold them down, only to find them nearly in place already. Another soldier grabbed an arm firmly, only to find the arm gentle and unresistant. "Father"—His voice spoke quietly and steadily—"Father, forgive them, for they don't know what they are doing."

"Strange criminal!" the soldier thought. "Almost seems as if he *wants* to die!"

They threw the cross roughly into a waiting hole, and Christ's body jerked cruelly against the spikes. The mob drew closer, unmindful of the darkness that had suddenly begun to settle over the landscape. "He thinks He's the Son of God, does He?" the mob jeered. "Why doesn't He do something to prove it?"

In the shadows beneath the cross a Figure stood unseen. An enormous ache, intensified by the passing of many centuries, welled up inside of Him. This "criminal"— taunted and despised—was His Son! Each stab of pain, evey gasp in that final life-and-death struggle registered on God's own suffering heart.

How precious was His Son, who, though equal with Himself, had given everything He had and was to reveal Their character! Against the backdrop of Satan's lies, the truth now stood forth clearly. Satan had claimed that God was selfish and oppressive, wanting everything for Himself. Yet in Jesus, God had given everything for His enemies.

In spite of the anguish, God's memory reached back, to a more peaceful time in the life of His Son—

The dust puffed up from beneath the Man's sandals and slid between His toes, mingling with the sweat. Shimmering heat waves made the horizon dance, and His face was dotted with moisture. It was high noon, and the road seemed endless. Wearily He sat down near a well shaded by a few junipers while His disciples—still with energy to spare, since they hadn't been continually giving to people as He had—went to buy food.

To be alone again, away from the crowds of needy and love-hungry people who tracked Him everywhere He went, was refreshing to Him. Yet His heart was still with them, longing to give more.

He glanced up to see a Samaritan woman approaching

the well with a jar. She pretended not to see him. After all, no self-respecting Jew would think of speaking to a hated Samaritan like her!

One glance flaunted in His face the advertisements she wore to be read by the men in her town. Yet with godlike perception, the Man saw more. Emptiness. Five former husbands. No comprehension of genuine love. Some might consider her as simply a thing to be misused until, worn out, all that remained would be to throw her out onto the garbage heap of human wreckage.

The Man's overflowing love and purity reached out to her, eager to set her free. How might she best accept help without feeling confronted? Ah? dignity—the need to be needed, the need to feel worthwhile. He could fulfull that need.

"Would you mind bringing me a drink of water? He asked courteously. His gentle voice startled her.

Almost without thinking, she responded, "How is it that You, a Jew, ask water from me, a Samaritan?" Skepticism lifted her eyebrows, suspicion gleamed in her eyes, surprise filled her voice.

Her question haunted the mind of God. In varied forms the question would grow so old— so deep. Again and again it would reveal the prejudices of each succeeding age: "What makes you think you can sit here, Nigger?" "Can't you take No for an answer, you good-fer-nothin' brat of a kid?" "Why did they move into our neighborhood anyway? Welfare people don't belong here."

Hatred. Burning deeply and warping minds with its heat. Bigoted hatred. Born of unjustified prejudice and maturing into division and cruelty. Hatred. The result of misunderstanding God.

This hatred, enshrouding an outcast woman, received a dash of water to quench its blistering flames one day. For a Man called God gave up His drink of water to give a

43

prostitute His message about His Father. When she left, His throat still burned, His stomach still growled, His feet still ached. But He was oblivious to it all.

Love. If only they could understand how much His Father loved them.

But for the sorrow of the cross, the Father would have remembered that day with absolute joy. His Son was just like Himself. Even as a man He so accurately painted God's portrait that Satan's lies were rapidly fading like the mirage they were.

There had been another day—another prostitute—a Jewess used by religious leaders and then condemned by them to die.

They had dragged her in before Jesus, where He stood teaching the people about His Father's love. Like the grating of a hacksaw, their voices marred His gracious words.

"This women here," the spokesman's voice rasped cruelly, "was caught in the act of adultery. We actually found her doing it! Now, Moses commanded that ones like her should be stoned. What do *You* say?"

Both the act and the question had been framed as a trap for Jesus. If only He were not so loving *and* so holy. These two qualities of God's character didn't seem to fit together in their minds. For weeks they had tried to find some excuse to condemn Him. Now they felt they had a chance. Either He would contradict what they believed the Old Testament taught about God, or He would admit that God was less loving than He claimed.

But Jesus did neither. Instead, like the Father whose heart He revealed, He quietly bent over and wrote something in the dust. Anxiously the leaders waited and wondered.

"Look! Aren't You listening?" They threw the words at the Man still bent over writing. "This woman ought to be stoned, and we want Your opinion on this matter!"

Calmly Jesus looked up and said, "Let the person among you who has never sinned throw the first stone."

Conviction poured over the accusers as they read their guilty secrets in the dust, and silently they crept away, leaving the woman at Jesus' feet.

She had flinched at Jesus' answer. Maybe *He* would throw the first stone. Surely one of the leaders would; they were always telling everyone how righteous they were. Terrified, she waited for the stones to crash into her body, hoping the first one would knock her out so she wouldn't feel the others. What would happen after that though? Would she meet an angry God? Right now, He seemed to bend over her, scowling like the religious leaders, brandishing a knife of judgment inches from her frightened face.

"Woman," the gentle voice inquired as she stood trembling to her feet, "where are your accusers?"

The quiet question slowed her pulse, and she looked around. A nearly deserted space stared back at her as she searched for the angry, cruel faces. Silence, like silence of a deep pond, swept over her. Was it real?

"Has no one condemned you?"

She looked at His face and saw kindly eyes. A smile greeted her. Compassionate lines blended with dignity— the two qualities seemed one. "No one, Sir," she replied.

"Then I don't condemn you either," He said.

The Father-God treasured that moment when love did what angry words could never do. Falling at His feet, the woman sobbed out her repentance, gratitude, and faith.

When she rose to her feet, she waited for more words. She was willing to listen to anything now. But His words were few and full of hope. "Go on from here," He said, "and be a new person."

Then there had been that day—a man—years of

illness—lying on a mat beside a pool that could supposedly heal him.

"You're a terrible sinner!" they had assured him thirty-eight years before when he had fallen ill. Not that such indictments were anything new, but their unfeeling words wounded him nonetheless.

When he had been taken to the pool of healing, he had hoped God would be merciful and help him get to the water first when it moved. If he were not first, someone else would be; and that person would be healed. Word was that every so often a heavenly hand moved the waters, and the first person to enter the pool after that was healed.

How often he had tried to get there first and failed. Sometimes he had waited tensely for hours, hoping that the next moment would be the moment he had longed for. When such a moment would finally come, he would flex his muscles and push with his chest, exerting everything he had to make his atrophying muscles respond. But always someone got there first—someone more healthy, apparently less sinful, and more worthy then he.

Sometimes the struggling didn't seem worth it. He knew he couldn't live much longer now. He would probably die before the waters moved again.

The apathy of resignation crept slowly over his wasting body and deteriorating mind and with it the urge to go to sleep for the last time. Or would he sleep only to awaken to the crimson face of an angry God about to visit hellish vengeance upon him? Such a picture made it difficult to sleep peacefully.

If only he could be healed. Yet he knew how sinful he'd been. Everyone knew it. God was simply punishing him for it all.

Outside, the voices of people floated to his ears. Everyone seemed to be going somewhere. Then he remembered: today was the Sabbath. No use to think of being healed for twenty-four hours. God would never think of healing anyone on His holy day, especially such a sinner as he.

Lifting his head, he looked toward the pool once more. Smooth and calm, the water seemed to mock him. He sighed, laid his head down again, and closed his eyes for a moment. Every cell in his body seemed to beg for rest.

Suddenly his eyelids lifted, and he saw a face bending over him. Never had he seen a face filled with such understanding, love, and genuine compassion.

"Would you like to be well?" The voice of the Man bending over him rang out clearly like a chime, playing a melody of love and hope.

Maybe this Man could help him. And yet—he remembered the many times he had tried and failed to reach the pool without anyone to help him. Surely this stranger dressed for Sabbath wouldn't be willing to stay until the next time the waters moved. Besides, he would probably die before then.

"Sir," he wearily explained, "there's no one to put me in the waters when they are moved. Before I can get there, someone else goes in." He felt too weak to say more and started to look away. But that face, so full of love, held his eyes.

"Get up," the quiet but authoritative voice invited, filling him with hope. "Pick up your bed and walk."

The Man's words penetrated his discouraged mind with an assurance that he could walk. Coupled with the trustworthy demeanor of the Man standing above him, those words conveyed the certainty of truthfulness and inspired trust in his heart. He believed—and stood up.

Picking up his bed, he turned to thank his benefactor, but the kind Man was gone. Alone, yet filled with overflowing joy, he lifted his right foot forward, then his left, then his right again. Soon he was almost running away from the pool, out to the street, toward the center of town. "Praise God!" he shouted. "Praise God!"

If only he could find someone to talk to about what had just happened! Ah, there were some men coming toward him now. And they were religious leaders. They would understand.

"Sirs," he announced excitedly, "the most wonderful thing just happened to me. I was lying there beside the pool of Bethesda and—"

Suddenly a forefinger stabbed at his chest. Surprised, he looked into long, scowling faces and into eyes that seemed to blaze with the lightning bolts of God's anger. "Why are you carrying your mat on the Sabbath?" they demanded. "Don't you know that it's against the law to carry any load on the Lord's holy day?"

Such words—which these religious leaders often repeated—stung the One who had made the Sabbath. For years at a time the day was totally ignored. Every time His people rejected Him they rejected His Sabbath. Then finally they would decide to keep the Sabbath. They would keep it so holy that they could not be faulted. But because they still ignored the Lord of the Sabbath, they could only find the day difficult to keep.

But they were determined. They would *force* themselves to obey. Rigorously they made rules and then rules to spell out the rules. As the list lengthened, God shuddered at these unbending, arbitrary rules.

How could they do this to His beautiful day, the memorial of the truth about Himself? How could they twist it around to represent a deity who not only made them especially miserable on that day but who would refuse to relieve a dying man's suffering because the day was "too holy." What blasphemy! As if God's holiness were too righteous to love, too exalted to stoop and serve!

But He wouldn't let their rules be the last word on the

Sabbath. Through Jesus and His followers He would show the truth about Himself and thus about His Sabbath. The people bent double under the weight of so many rules would know that God would forgive and heal a man on that day, setting him free from suffering. They would see that holiness equals love—that royalty seeks to serve.

Another scene. Evening—an upstairs room—a pan of water—twelve men—their Creator.

Scowling men all but shoved their way into the room that night. Grumbling silently to themselves, their angry thoughts surged and roiled through their selfish minds.

"Why does John have to be such a big shot?"

"Peter should learn to keep his mouth shut. I can just hear him boasting if Jesus makes him first in the kingdom."

"Thomas is certainly no leader, in spite of what he claims. I just wish he would realize that I could do the job better."

Hot silence suffocated the peace in the room and stifled their love. Nearby a pan sat empty, waiting to be filled. Peter looked at John questioningly. Who would do the customary job of washing their feet before they ate? John looked at James. James looked at Philip. Philip shrugged.

The Man sat waiting as if apart from the others. Quietly He studied their faces, especially one face etched with rebellion. Judas. Grasping, miserly, thieving Judas. Soon he would betray His God for so little. The Man's mind clouded thinking of the one created in His own image who would soon hang himself in despair from a tree. How can you destroy yourself, Judas? His heart called out.

Moments lengthened in the heat of the silent mini-war. Slowly Jesus stood up and took off His coat. Then, tying a towel around His waist, He filled the empty pan with water and knelt in front of Judas.

A universe watched and remembered. From back across the years an earlier but similar picture returned to

49

mind. Once before God had knelt to serve. Taking mud in His hands, He had shaped it into the first man. But then the world had been perfect and full of love. Now it was ugly, and the hearts of the men here in this place were filled with almost everything but love.

But the same God who had worked with His Father to fashion every creature now lifted up the feet of His betrayer and washed the dust gently away.

The universe framed that moment. Framed it in contrast to Satan's claim that God was selfish and proud. Framed it in the center of the heavens as an immortal picture of service.

Moments later Jesus spoke the caption for that picture: "Anyone who has seen me has seen the Father." John 14:9, NIV.

Disciples, you've seen Me give Myself to people— healing them, relieving their suffering, teaching them about My Father. Yet in all of that, You have seen the Father just as fully as if He were Me.

Now, beneath the cross, the Father looks up at His Son, convulsed in pain. Their oneness has not diminished with the last thirty-three years. His Son is no less God now that He is also fully man. The Father's heart longs to reach out to His Son and demonstrate that oneness. Instead, He lets the cross bear the message He can't give in words:

Universe, now you can see how much I love My creatures. Now you know that I did not create men for selfish reasons, to make them suffer. In giving up My beloved Son, I give Myself in sacrifice. There is nothing more I can give. I've given all I have.

Chapter 7

Darkness, like a mourner's dress, draped itself over the cross. At a time when the sun usually beat down on them, the people groped through a smothering blackness more intense than midnight.

In that darkness the Father still stood beneath the cross, waiting. He was with His Son and yet, to His Son, He was far away. To His Son, the distance between Them spanned the black ribbon of distrust stretching between heaven and earth.

Again God remembered the day that the ribbon had begun to unroll. Slyly, beautifully, but without love, the deceiver had said to Eve, "I know God *said* if you eat of this tree you will die. But you won't. God has lied to you!"

Was God a liar? If God was a liar, He could not be God. And even if the accusation was false, nothing He could say would correct the picture. Though He knew His words were true, no claim of His honesty could prove it. His very best words and most persuasive arguments would be considered lies.

Had He allowed Adam and Eve or Satan and his fellow rebels to die the ultimate death—that final result of distrust and rebellion—His words would have been proven true. Yet the rest of His creatures would have worshiped Him in fear. They had never seen anyone die before—even the death of worn-out bodies, let alone that final death. How could they understand that even that final death was the inevitable result of sin and that He hadn't arbitrarily executed His rebels?

So with infinite patience, God had waited until He could demonstrate that death in His Son and thus prove His word to be true.

Meanwhile, waiting had meant risking more of Satan's lies. Before the dark ribbon had stretched very far with the years, Satan picked up his hate-filled paintbrush. Dipping it into his ugliest colors, he began to retouch the pictures of God's interactions with mankind. A smear here, a darker shading there, and God's most merciful, freedom-giving actions appeared vengeful, arbitrary and cruel.

With a pang God remembered the Flood. It had been so like the flood of rebellion and cruelty that rose within Adam's descendants until it overflowed into chaos. Should He have let them destroy each other? He wanted to save as many as possible. In mercy He had to let those die who refused to go into the ark, in order to save any at all. He had given them plenty of time, evidence, and freedom to decide whether or not they wanted to be saved. Their dying had been their own choice.

Yet Satan thrust his fist still higher and roared across God's universe, "What a tyrannical despot! Why even try to live at all! See how He loves suffering and death!"

The Tower of Babel, that needless symbol of distrust, stretched toward heaven's face and spoke the consequences of Satan's lies. "How can we know for sure that God will keep His promise not to drown the world again in a flood? He could rain us out tomorrow! We can't trust Him; we will save ourselves."

Then there lingered in God's mind those tense, complaint-filled years when the Israelites—whining like small children—dragged their rebellious feet across the desert. Rudely and repeatedly they lashed out at God's love with their distrust. Impatiently they refused to listen to His messages except under extreme pressure. The trials they brought on themselves they blamed upon God. When the water ran out, they screamed in paranoid anger, "You've brought us out here to kill us!" Though God suffered in their sufferings, they claimed He didn't care.

Satan's lies about God rang relentlessly in their ears. "Look how God punishes people when they disobey Him! Just look at Korah, Dathan, and Abiram and at the people who died from snakebites. If you don't obey Him, He kills you—makes you suffer. Who wants to worship a god who enjoys suffering!"

It didn't matter that each of the situations demanded firm action and that God was doing His best to help them understand the terrible things sin did to them. The people preferred to listen to Satan's lies rather than the truth, and they turned to other gods whose characters were even worse than Satan's pictures of the true God. They worshiped Baal, who degraded human beings to mere bodies and required cruel self-abuse to appease his anger. They bowed to Moloch as he grasped their small children in his fire-filled hands.

Deep in the shadows of their superstitious minds, the real God pleaded with tears clogging His voice, "I'm not like that. I love you. Please come back to Me." But the people's ears, dulled by angry imprecations, heard only faint whispers.

Finally the whispers become so faint that they could no longer hear the undertones of love. Even when they threw away their gods and pretended to worship the one true God, He became to them little better than their former gods. What they viewed as His unreasonable wrath seemed to burn constantly against them. Their God became a cruel punisher of all sinners. Every illness, accident, or disaster they viewed as a stroke of the cruel, searing finger of God's wrath. Every person thus smitten was shunned and despised as a terrible sinner.

And then Jesus came—the representative of this God who was blamed for all the suffering in the world—and He healed the sick and rescued minds tortured by Satan. Paralytics leaped with joy. Blind men kissed His feet—feet they could see. The emotionally unstable walked away upright because they looked above the frowns of people into His understanding eyes. Even the dead lived again, for He turned graveside tears into smiles of unspeakable joy.

Slowly the tables turned. The One blamed for all the suffering in the universe became the Suffering One. A universe watched as, with all his ingenuity, Satan harassed their God. "He's down here in human flesh where I can reach Him," he gloated, "and I'm going to get Him!"

Through the minds of evil men, Satan worked to destroy Christ's demonstrations and teachings about God. Maliciously the people twisted His words, like so many rubber bands and than snapped them back in His face. Their God was not this loving and honest. Jesus wasn't angry enough, mean enough, unconcerned enough; and they rejected Him. For how, they questioned, could such a completely gracious Person be God?

At Satan's instigation they came in a cruel mob to seize Him like an escaped murderer. How ironic that they should treat the One filled with love like a criminal! Roughly they led Him through the dark, winding streets to the temple. After a mock trial, dragging on through a night filled with bitter insults and base torture, they led Him— bleeding, hungry, thirsty—to the hill where He now hung from the cross.

Through clouded eyes a horrified universe watched as the liar who had blamed suffering and death on God tried to rend His Son's life and crack His goodness.

But even more terrible than all the physical and emotional abuse heaped upon Him was that long, dark ribbon of separation that would, in the end, take Jesus' life.

A massive sob shook the frame of the Father below. Now He must completely withdraw His presence from His Son. He must treat Him as if He were all the people who had believed Satan's lies and misrepresented God. By treating Him this way God would demonstrate that sin does cause death, that God had not lied to Adam and Eve when He said they would die, that His commands really were the best way to life.

Now He would step back and let the blackness cover His Son. He would give His Son up.

The thick blackness fell—choking, smothering. The Son reached out to feel that familiar Presence—that warm, comforting Presence that had always been with Him. But the Presence was gone. A wave of horror swept over Him. His Father. His Father was gone! What if He never saw Him again? Sin and suffering were so terrible. Satan's lies were so unnecessary. And to be treated as if He had believed them all—

Would His death and separation have to be eternal to prove that sin could only destroy sinners? Maybe He would never again feel His Father's loving arms around Him. Maybe that gentle smile would never again fill His life. Maybe—

One by one, like darts of flaming steel, Satan hurled doubts into His mind. "All Your life You've been telling others how loving and kind your Father is and how He loves to forgive sinners. Look where You are now! How do You know He really loves you? How do You know He's not angry with You—so angry that You'll never see Him again?"

As the thoughts surged through His mind, the pain in His

heart grew intense. The darkness sank over Him—hot and stifling. Bolts of lightning streaked toward Him as if thrust from an angry hand.

"God's wrath has fallen upon Him," voices below intoned. "God's vengeance is destroying Him because He claimed to be God. We knew He was too gracious to be God. God isn't like that."

On the cross, the Son gasped for breath. Tensely He hung, His mind reaching out for the loving presence of His Father. But death crouched motionless, waiting to pounce on Him. Inside His chest the pain gripped His heart like a vice.

Beneath the cross the Father's heart seemed to rend with His Son's. How—how could He give Him up? How could He let His own beloved Son go? The suffering—could He go through with it? Sobs emerged from somewhere deep within Him. If only He could reach out once more to reassure His Son. If only He could bathe His bloody forehead. If only—

Oh why, why, why? Why this suffering?

"My God!" His Son's voice seemed to echo the Father's thoughts.

"My God!" Usually His Son called Him "Father," not "My God." The distance—would it never end? The suffering—how much longer would it go on?

"Why—why have you forsaken Me?"

That eternal question rang out across the timeless space to grasp the black ribbon of separation and begin the work of tearing it to shreds. For in that question was an answer. God was not murdering His own Son. He was merely forsaking Him, as He would have to forsake incurable sinners at the end. God was not the arbitrary deity Satan pictured Him to be. Sin—and the inevitable separation it brought—was the destroying agent.

God's wrath, which had fallen on His Son, would no

longer be seen by His loyal creatures as a senseless, deranged anger venting stored impatience on the wicked. Now they would know that there was simply no better word to describe His hatred of the sin that destroyed His once-beautiful creatures.

Now they would see that He hadn't lied to Adam and Eve when He warned them of death. They would know that God felt deeply about sin because He loved sinners and didn't want them to be destroyed.

In that terrible moment, the Son on the cross remembered. He remembered nights when He had clung to His Father in prayer. He remembered days when They walked together. He remembered the love that had filled His heart as He worked to share the truth. He *knew* His Father. And He knew His Father *was* love.

In spite of the darkness and separation, Jesus could say what Adam and Eve and their descendants had failed to when confronted with Satan's lies. His muscles stretched taut, His heart rending with the pain of saying good-bye to His Father, Jesus could still say, "I can trust Him."

"It is finished!" His voice, triumphant with victory, rang through the universe like tolling of a great cathedral bell. With the joy of knowing that through His death the universe would know the truth about His Father, Jesus bowed His head and died.

Beneath the cross, the Father knelt and echoed, "It is finished." Now He thought to Himself, I've given all the evidence needed to win men back to Myself. Now men and woman won't have to die this death because, by showing them how correct I was about sin, I now have the right to save them. Now I can forgive those who turn from Satan's lies to the truth about Me without My universe assuming I've condoned their sins. Now only those who reject this evidence clearly shown by the cross will have to die the final death.

At last! His mind raced on. At last I've been shown to be both upright and merciful. Satan can no longer say that those attributes are in opposition. They never have been; the cross proves it. I have won My case, and the truth will ever conquer! Many will be saved through knowing Me as I really am.

Through His tears the Father saw a rainbow stretching out across the vastness of space. The cross now stood as a promise of tomorrow. For tomorrow heaven would celebrate as it had at the end of creation week. To that Sabbath day a new dimension would be added—celebration of God's victory over Satan's lies.

While Jesus rested in the tomb in the peaceful sleep of death, all God's loyal creatures would raise their voices in joy and praise. Yes, tomorrow would be a high day—a token of that future Sabbath of eternal rest.

Chapter 8

New leaves glisten softly in the light, trembling gently in a quiet breeze. Eyes twinkling in mischief, a fox dashes down a hill, his tail fluffed out. Behind him leaps a happy cougar playing tag. A woolly ewe bleats happily at the lion looking down at her. Sticking out his massive tongue, the big cat licks a gentle kiss on the sheep's forehead.

God smiles as again He walks in the cool time of the day. The soft light reminds Him of that morning long ago when springtime dew clung to the foliage of the garden and predawn darkness hovered over the tomb. There, in the night, two armies of angels waited. One army, composed of Satan's fellow rebels, had enlisted human soldiers to help guard the tomb. Tensely they had waited, hoping that the tomb would remain sealed forever. If Jesus could just be kept inside, Satan would win. Everyone would believe that God was indeed angry with His Son—so angry that He would refuse even to resurrect Him. They would conclude that the wrath that had fallen upon Jesus was cruel and totally out of harmony with God's love.

Only if Jesus rose again would the universe have evidence that one great purpose of the cross was to reveal that God would only destroy sinners by giving them up to the natural consequences of their rebellion. If Satan could just hold Jesus in death, he could proclaim that God had not won His case at the cross.

The other army also waited on guard, but with joyous excitement. Would the night never end? Soon—soon, they would be able to—

An intensely brilliant light suddenly flooded the landscape. Blinded, the soldiers fell senseless to the moist ground, and the demons scattered in terror. The highest angel of heaven reached down a mighty hand, and the stone in front of the tomb rolled away like a marble.

Eagerly God's angels waited for the signal. All Sabbath they had anticipated that moment when they could share the news with Christ. As soon as they saw His face, radiant with resurrection light, they shouted, "You've won! You've made it clear to us who is right, and we no longer have any sympathy with Satan's lies. They are absolutely false!"

The radiance of their joy beamed more brightly from the Father's face. At last! His Son was coming home. He was coming home as a conqueror free of suffering.

Yet, not all suffering would end now. As long as there were people on the earth to win back to Himself, God would have to wait to end suffering completely. Every person on earth must hear the truth about God that had been revealed on Calvary.

As Jesus' early followers received the truth about God, they eagerly raced to the others to explain why Jesus had come and died. Joyously they preached that the same gracious Person who had walked among them, healing and teaching the people, had promised to return to earth.

The news swept from home to home, from synagogue to synagogue: "Jesus is God in human flesh, and not only did He die that we might be saved, but He rose again and is now beside the Father. Now He is preparing a place for us where we can live when He comes to take us to heaven."

Nevertheless, not everyone reached toward the light to

let it warm them. The religious leaders who had spat angry words at Jesus now tried to snuff out His followers' lives. They imprisoned some, only to find them rejoicing at being permitted to share Jesus' sufferings. Those they scourged remembered His floggings. When thrown out of the synagogues, believers praised God that they were part of His universe-wide family.

Then the stones fell on Stephen, a young leader. As those stones carved from hearts of stone crushed his bones and splattered his blood against the ground, Stephen echoed Jesus' words: "Father, don't hold this sin against them."

But even those gracious words fell with a dull thud upon the stony hearts of a rebellious nation. For centuries God had called them "My people." Through them He had worked to help them reveal Himself to the world. But repeatedly they had only misrepresented Him, and now the stony-hearted nation could no longer hear His voice. As a nation there was nothing more God could do for her, though He would still try to save her individuals whose hearts had not turned to stone.

So hard were the stony hearts that not even tears could soften them. God could remember standing unseen with Jesus just a few weeks earlier on the steps of the temple. "O Jerusalem, Jerusalem," His Son had mourned, "how often I have longed to gather your people together in My arms, but you wouldn't let Me." His tears had fallen on the stony hearts—had fallen and run off.

They mingled again later with the stones that fell on the suffering Stephen. In the silence that followed his dying prayer, angels wondered, "Will suffering never end? Will truth die on earth as Stephen did?"

But one watched Stephen die whose heart had not hardened so completely that God couldn't melt it in love. God remembered the day He had met Saul on his way to persecute believers in the truth. Dramatic though the confrontation was, Saul recognized a loving God, who gently asked, "Why are you persecuting Me? It's hard on you to kick against the evidences of truth."

Saul became Paul—a torch of courage. Never before had any Bible writer proclaimed so fully that Jesus lived and died to vindicate God's character. No one had written so beautifully about love or had understood so fully God's wrath, as had Paul.

Under his leadership, truths about God raced out to envelop the world. Torches sprang up everywhere, reducing Satan's lies to ashes. Even though persecution sped after the light to blot it out, the light only sped faster.

But before the light could completely conquer, Satan began campaigning with an old lie about God put into a new framework. "Sure," he sneered, "God showed that He was not vengeful and cruel on the cross. He showed how eager He is to forgive. But what about His laws? Nobody but Jesus ever showed that they were anything but arbitrary and legalistic. Even the cross could be taken to mean that His laws are inconsistent with His graciousness. Therefore the cross invalidates His laws."

Paul, John, and James had earlier contradicted his claims. They had stated that the demonstration of God's character that enabled sinners to trust Him again had not done away with the law. Rather, such faith enabled them to joyfully keep God's laws of liberty. By demonstrating on the cross the natural results of breaking His laws, Jesus had shown that they were reasonable and deserved to be kept.

In spite of apostolic efforts, the lies crept in, moldy and damp, nearly extinguishing the light. Finally the darkness grew more intense than the darkness before the cross. And in that darkness, a longsuffering God waited to show Himself. "Oh why," He mourned, "do they always turn to Satan's lies? And now, when they have the light of the cross? Will this suffering continue needlessly?"

He knew the answer; He knew how long the suffering would stretch out. Again, only time and suffering would give people adequate opportunities and evidence to decide what was the real truth about Himself.

Mobilizing all his slyness, Satan particularly attacked the heart of God's law—His gift of the seventh-day Sabbath. The gift that should have most reminded mankind of God's graciousness had become twisted to represent a cruel god.

Having warped the Sabbath's meaning, Satan proceeded to persuade Christians that this day could no longer represent the God of the cross and that they must therefore keep another day. Gradually listening to him, they chose another day on which to worship—a day they felt would more accurately represent God and yet be popular with non-Christians.

God wept at the change He'd forseen so long before. A substitute day would soon mean a substitute God. "Oh, why can't they see," He cried, "that the problem of legalism does not center around the day. The problem is that people have believed Satan's lies and have warped the meaning of the Sabbath. To change My day—a day reflecting My graciousness, which won the victory over Satan's lies—is to concede that those lies were really true."

God was right. Instead of the Sabbath substitution making their God appear more gracious, it gradually led to their viewing Him as more tyrannical than ever before. Human laws reflecting Satan's view of God replaced God's laws. Jesus became an exacting judge ready to inflict punishment on those who didn't do enough good works to merit salvation. The suffering of the cross appeared insufficient to appease a God who now seemed cruel and vengeful. Therefore—so it was said—one must afflict oneself to find favor with God.

Fathers beat their backs until the blood flowed. Mothers crawled long, weary miles in penance. Small children cried as sharp stones cut into their knees. Heaven mourned as the message of God's graciousness—so vigorously clarified by Paul—disappeared along with the Sabbath.

Then in the superstitious darkness Satan gleefully picked up his paintbrush again. Dipping it deep into the colors of his own evil nature, he began to paint the most horrifying caricatures of God. A cruel, vicelike hand, flinging souls into a terrible inferno of blasting wrath. A purple, bloated face in which gleamed rage-filled eyes. And while he played psychedelic lights over the picture, Satan also played his favorite acid-rock record, filling the imaginations of millions with the shrieks and screams of sinners.

But in the middle of it all, Satan's god sat back, smiling hideously and sometimes laughing with cruel delight whenever this eternal punishment called hell was presented.

With moist eyes and a pained heart, the gracious God who had given everything He had to reveal Himself as a God of fairness and love watched Satan's portrayal capture the minds of multitudes. Men shuddered in terror, women fainted in church pews, and children screamed in their sleep at nightmares filled with flames and horrible faces.

In horror God cried out, "Why this suffering, this needless suffering? Why have they forgotten the message of the cross?"

Meanwhile, church leaders banned Bibles from the homes of their people, explaining that "only the wise and those especially close to God can correctly understand and interpret this revelation." Without access to the only book containing the real truth about God, people sank even lower into the darkness—deep, mysterious darkness.

Religion became a list of rites to perform, rounds of

self-abusing punishments to inflict, and meaningless words to repeat. God became so cold and heartless, in their view, that it took Jesus and all the saints in history to persuade Him to throw a crumb of mercy down to the most pious Christian.

No one breathes freely in such a system. Children had little choice about whether or not they wanted to worship this kind of God. Born into clutching arms of this corrupt system, they had precious little opportunity to question its validity. Any question might offend their capricious god, who abhorred all questions—especially the question "Why?"

The loyal universe looking on realized that abandoning God's laws—even one commandment—would result in suffering. Without God's gentle guidelines, disorder and confusion concerning His character would result. For the law was nothing less than a transcript of His attributes.

As the darkness of that chaos deepened on the earth, angels studied truth and error. Only here and there, hidden in remote mountain or wilderness retreats, could they find dots of light shining forth from those who had not given up the truth about God. Would the light ever shine again as it had at the cross?

Even in the midnight blackness a man was rising who would dare to ask that disturbing question, "Why?" Like a star in the night, his answer would open minds to more light and more answers about God's character. Others would follow, until the night would turn to dawn.

Chapter 9

The giant tree stretches out huge leafy branches over the One pausing thoughtfully beneath it. Already the dark night, with all its sorrow and suffering, seems far away. And it will never come again!

God's eyes glow as He remembers that star which, like the morning star, sent out the first rays of truth as a preamble to dawn. His name was John Wycliffe, and from his pen came the first English translation of the Bible designed for the common people. No longer was the Bible hidden away and reserved only for scholars and church leaders. Now the masses too could learn the truth about God that had previously been submerged in Satan's lies.

Fingers of light from the rising sun followed the star and reached into countless homes. Gradually, the people adjusted to the unaccustomed brightness. "Can it be," they asked as they rubbed their eyes, "that we too may ask questions? Is it possible that we can interpret the Bible for ourselves? Is it true that we don't need to make God love us—that He has shown Himself already willing to forgive us?"

The Reformers, as they later came to be called, studied the revelation about God in the Bible and uncovered there much of His freedom, love, and graciousness. Eagerly, a Father-God watched, as home after home opened its doors and windows to a now more compassionate picture of Deity. Carefully He soothed burdened hearts and darkened minds with the news that He did not require the penance of anyone in order to save him. Gently he relieved imaginations terrified by the picture of an angry tyrant, offering in its place the picture of a God who loved the world even as it rejected Him.

Just as God was ready to fling the bright rays of this sunlight to the world, giant hands reached out to push them back. Those who had become captivated by God's graciousness were seized by those cruel hands and commanded to give up their faith. When they would not, the cruel hands dragged them off to dreadful fates.

Some waited as flames crept slowly up their bodies and seared their flesh. Others sat in working the oars day and night with little to eat until they died of exhaustion. Others shuddered in pain as the rack stretched their muscles taut. Still others were dismembered by roaring mobs.

Above it all, an empathetic God wept and longed to end the horrors below. The eternal question that had ruptured His Son's heart at the cross burst forth again: "Why this suffering? Why this suffering *in My name?* I am not a persecuting God. Their god is a cruel tyrant who loves suffering and vengeance, and they've become just like him."

Yet through His tears, He could see dawn's fingers still reaching across the sky. The suffering of His people would only serve to make truth more obvious.

He watched as new bodies of believers arose, each claiming the Bible as its only authority and guide and claiming to have uncovered the truth—all of it.

God winced at such claims, for He knew how much truth still remained to be discovered beneath the rubbish of error.

Then smaller groups sprang up, releasing more light and

revealing a more gracious picture of God. Their God was freedom-giving—a God who wanted them to worship Him without tedious forms and ceremonies. Their God never asked that children and babies be baptized as Christians without the opportunity of choosing Him for themselves.

But some of the religious groups that followed the Reformers were unwilling to accept these and other new truths. God couldn't be *that* gracious! How could one serve Him and be that free? Slamming shut the doors of their minds and churches to freedom, they began to persecute some of the newer, small groups.

Patiently still in control, God watched the fog roll in— misty and damp. In that fog, religious groups clashed and struggled. As time went by many different churches and denominations raised steeples to the sky, claiming to have all of the truth. They seemed willing now to give freedom to each other.

But God knew that the sun had not yet fully risen. Fog still hovered over the churches, and no one church had all of the truth. Much was still hidden. Unless something happened soon, the night—filled with superstition— would return.

God pondered a date He had chosen long before Jesus was born. A date associated with the restoring of truth and human lives. A date inextricably bound up with the very heart of things—the most holy place of the heavenly sanctuary. The sanctuary represented Him as He really is. But in the most holy place could be seen the truth about Himself in its purest form. There, everything pointed to God and His true character.

From the most holy place God would soon be able to release a renewed understanding of what had happened at the cross. Through years of misunderstanding, the cross had come to be seen as an appeasement sacrifice to satisfy God's cold, unbending justice. This justice, preachers thundered from pulpits, would someday punish those who rejected the cross by casting them into a hideous, everlasting inferno of wrath.

How God longed for them to grasp the real meaning of the cross. But now, starting with the date He had set, He could begin to show them more fully the truth about His justice.

God took a breath deep with anticipated joy. He would teach His people that His justice and love were nothing less than the glory of His righteous character. In that light, mercy and justice blended together. How well the most holy place symbolized this!

Through the ministry of the most holy place, God would teach the truth that He did not delight in suffering. Death was not eternal hell or heaven. Death due to old age, accidents, and disease was but a sleep. Both the righteous and the wicked would be raised from that death. And even the final death of the wicked would not mean everlasting punishment, but complete annihilation—the natural result of sin.

God paused as His mind leaped back over the years to the day He had given Moses those ten commands that spelled love. Well He had known that Satan's final attack against His character and government would center around whether or not His law deserved the obedience of His creatures in every respect. Satan claimed that the law was unreasonable and arbitrary in light of the cross—especially the Sabbath commandment commanding worship on the seventh day.

But God would soon be enlightening His people concerning the law. Satan's charges against the Sabbath would be forever refuted, for His people would no longer regard the Sabbath as a legalistic day in which God looked for ways to make them miserable. They would learn that above all His other commands, the Sabbath reflected His graciousness. In fact, it stood as a memorial to the truth about His character. Joyfully His people would keep the Sabbath in celebration of their Creator's victories over Satan's lies. Their correct observance of this day would reveal that they had found Him worthy of their trust.

The date was now not far off for all of this. Somehow and soon He must awaken the interest of His people, drawing them away from their confusion of doctrine to Himself.

He knew how He would do it. He had planned it many centuries ago. Hidden in the prophecies of the Old Testament was a gift containing a special date. All this time He had waited for the right setting, place, and time for the date to be revealed.

But He must find a listening man—calm and intelligent—to open this special gift.

He found His man—a middle-aged farmer named William Miller. As he studied the Bible, Miller found that not a little had been written about Jesus' plans to come back and take His people to heaven. Digging into the prophecies, Miller discovered that the event was to take place soon. In fact, as a result of careful study in Daniel, he concluded that Christ would come to cleanse His sanctuary (which he assumed was the earth) on a day foretold in the Bible. Through prayer and accurate calculation, Miller and others finally set the date as October 22, 1844.

God's hidden gift had been discovered and unwrapped! And though they had misunderstood the event, He also knew that in the disappointment that would follow when He did not appear on October 22, they would be driven back to the Bible. Already expelled from their churches because of their belief that He would come, they would cling to the Bible alone for guidance and comfort. And through the Bible they would uncover the truths about God that Satan had hidden away for centuries.

On October 22, 1844, God, His Son, and His Spirit entered upon the special ministry of the most holy place. At last They could unleash the final rays of light. At last the noonday sun would shine!

And though They knew that Their people would not understand every truth all at once, eventually the sun would reach high noon. For as they saw the light more clearly, that light would etch into their minds the true picture of God, until they became like Him. They would not be able to help it, because truth, when loved and admired, can only restore a person into God's image.

Then the law that revealed God's character would also reveal His character as displayed in His people. God couldn't wait for the day when He could turn at last to the waiting universe and exclaim: "Satan said it couldn't happen, but look at My people now! Here are those who have completely rejected all of Satan's lies. Look how the truth has set them free! They are ready to answer any questions about Me, both by their teaching and by the way their lives reflect Me. I can trust them to defend My reputation to the end."

"Oh, if only it could be soon!" God's heart longed to see the light shed quickly so He could come again. "Oh, if only they would learn the truth and then spread it eagerly to the world. The world would soon have enough evidence to decide fully for or against Me. Then I could come again.

"Nevertheless," God added, "I will wait. I will not overpower them or force them to decide under unnecessary pressure. I will give them time to decide. I want as many as possible to be saved."

Time. How well God knew that more time would mean more suffering. He suddered as His mind swept forward through the future. The Civil War and racial prejudice. Kaiser Wilhelm and World War I. Hitler. Six million Jews.

71

Concentration camps. Vietnam. Cambodia. And the countless accidents, famines, murders, and disease. Little children crying naked in the streets beside their dead mothers. Teenagers throwing themselves from tall buildings, trying to escape suffering. Selfishness and greed splitting millions of families apart and leaving children emotionally maimed for life.

Yes, time would mean more suffering, for there was no other way. The time that meant freedom and salvation for His creatures would also bring deep suffering to them.

Time means My suffering, too, God thought. Not all My suffering took place at the cross. The cross was simply a description of all the heartbreak I have endured and will yet endure for people. I feel it all with them; I feel it more than they do, because I love more!

But—and God's joy arched across the vault of heaven—suffering will not go on forever. Soon My Son will go back. It's October 22, 1844! The beginning of the last lap of time. The beginning of the final triumph of truth. The beginning of the end of suffering!

In the quiet coolness, God lingers to savor the sweetness of an earth now fully renewed. No pain or sorrow can be traced here. No more need now to cry out, "Why this suffering?" And it's not because the question had been fully answered, but because the problem of suffering has been solved.

Just a few days earlier, He had raised the wicked back to life. Then before the entire universe—before every person who has ever lived—He had unrolled a panorama of the entire history of the great controversy over Satan's lies about His character. No bias, no hiding of the truth. Just the facts of history.

But the evidence had been so overwhelming that all—righteous and unrighteous—had knelt and declared that

God had always been right—and had also been right about themselves.

The righteous had waited to see what the wicked would do next. In fury, they had rushed upon one another and tried to destroy each other. God had looked around to see if anyone wanted this suffering to go on. No one did. They understood now, in the light of Jesus' death, what the destruction of the wicked would be like.

Slowly, the heartbreak of centuries distilling in His tears, God let His glory consume them. There was nothing more He could do for the wicked, and He could no longer spare them from the natural results of their rebelliousness. But as He gave them up, His message to them was clear:

"When you were young, I loved you and called you to respond to My love. But no matter what I did, you despised Me and chose to go away.

"Because I loved you and respected your freedom, I let you have your choice. I longed to have you reconsider the truth and decide that I deserved your love and faith. But although I gave you everything I had to win you back, you chose to reject Me completely.

"Now I must allow you to be destroyed, for there is nothing more I can do for you. Yet, how can I do it? I created you for happiness, for freedom, for eternity—not for this! How can I give you up?

"I love you! I only wanted you to live with Me in joy and freedom forever. Now I must let you go. I will always wish you had chosen to trust Me.

"Please understand—it is not because I hate you that I'm doing this, but because I love you! I could let you cruelly destroy yourselves. Or I could force you to live in My presence, forever tortured by My love.

"But I won't do that. I will let you choose to be destroyed, because I am merciful. It is My last chance to show you that I love you!"

God remembers now how the universe that remained after the destruction of the wicked praised God that His justice had been shown to be so merciful and gracious. Yes, God thought to Himself, the questions about Me have all been answered, and in those answers the problem of suffering has been solved.

Suddenly He lifts His voice in song—a song sweeping through the trees and gathering His people to Himself. "May we celebrate?" He asks. "May we celebrate on the seventh day of each week the truth that won you back to Me?"

"Oh, please! We'd love to!" Their answers reverberate with praise across the universe.

Yes, it's Sabbath again. And forever that day will stand as a memorial to the Creator who has shown Himself to be fully and forever love. A memorial to the God who never caused pain and anguish, but who allowed it because there was no other satisfactory way. A memorial to the God who, in His own deepest agony, cried out, "Why this suffering?"

And from Sabbath to Sabbath—and every day in between—it will be joyfully remembered that the truth about God, like a mighty knife, has forever severed the dark ribbon of Satan's lies.

Epilogue

The stretcher, white and sterile, blots out everything but her fears. As the screaming of the siren slices through the air, she wonders. Why her husband? A heart attack—now? God, where are you? Her thoughts scream out with the ambulance. Don't You care? Why have You let this happen?

Maybe you've asked similar questions. Maybe you too have cried out, "Why this suffering?"

In this book we haven't attempted a complex answer to the problem of human suffering. In fact, we haven't attempted an answer at all. Instead, we've simply told a story—the story of a God who did not cause the suffering. A God who, though He hates suffering, allowed it because there was ultimately no other way suffering could end without destroying our freedom.

But while there is no real and satisfactory reason for suffering, there is a solution to the woes of humanity. That solution is not to be found in a theory or a drug cop-out or in a frantic effort to forget. Rather, it lies in finding God completely worthy of our love and trust. If we let Him be the Friend to us He longs to be, suffering will still confront us. But with Him, the suffering will be bearable, sometimes even beautiful. And for us, it won't continue forever. Suffering will end.

In the preceding chapters we've focused on how trustworthy God is. From this story of His sufferings we hope you've found Him to be One who understands your sufferings. He truly feels them with you.

In a very personal way He wants to share Himself with you. He wants to open to you His love and security. With Him you can still walk through deep valleys of anguish. Yet you will have Him walking beside you.

You are free to choose for or against Him. Free to follow Satan's tangled ribbons of lies or to accept the truth God has shared about Himself. Free to suffer with or without Him.

If you reject Him, He will suffer far more than you will. He will feel that tearing pain of saying an eternal good-bye, the realization of what you'll go through without Him, the gnawing thought that your separation from Him was so needless.

Through His tears, He'll call after you, "Don't you care that I love you? I have so much freedom and joy to share with you! Why are you rejecting Me? Why must you die? Why? Why?"

References

These sections are based on the following Bible passages:

Flashback Eden
    Genesis 1; 2; 3.
    Exodus 33:18 to 34:7.
    Job 38:7.
    Isaiah 14:12-14.
    Ezekiel 20:12, 20; 28:12-19.
    Revelation 12:7-12.

Flashback Bethlehem
    Genesis 4:1-11; 18.
    Exodus 25; 33:18 to 34:7; cf. Exodus 24:17; Hebrews 12:29.
    1 Samuel 3; 8.
    Hosea 1; 3.
    Luke 2:1-20.
    John 1:1-18.
    Philippians 2:6-11.
    Hebrews 1; 9:19-21; 10:1-18.

Flashback Calvary
    Genesis 3:1-7; 11:1-9.
    Matthew 27.
    Mark 15.
    Luke 23.
    John 4:1-38; 5:1-13; 8; 13; 14:1-11.
    Romans 1; 3; 4:25.
    2 Corinthians 5:11-21.

Flashback New Eden
    Daniel 7; 8.
    Matthew 27:57 to 28:8.
    Mark 16:1-6.
    Acts 7:54 to 8:3; 9.
    Revelation 2; 3; 10; 20; 21; 22.

Other Books You Will Enjoy

Herbert Douglass,   *The End*

C. Mervyn Maxwell,   *God Cares*

Ken McFarland,   *Gospel Showdown*

Jean Sheldon,   *Sharing Jesus*

Morris Venden,   *Good News/Bad News*

Morris Venden,   *The Return of Elijah*

Dick Winn,   *If God Won the War, Why
                Isn't It Over?*

Penny Wheeler,   *More Than Harps Of Gold*

Penny Wheeler,   *The Beginning*

E. G. White,   *Facing Life's Record*

E. G. White,   *Message From Calvary*

Published by

Pacific Press Publishing Association
Mountain View, California